What people are saying

A Simple Faith in a Complicated World

If you want to be told what you should believe don't read this book! Kate McNally, after discarding the strict dogmatic religion of her childhood, takes us on her journey of discovery, as she explores "the faith *of* Jesus rather than the faith *about* Jesus."

Like many of us, from her first experience of a Quaker meeting, she knew she had come home. For non-Quakers she explains Quakerism so simply and clearly. "In the end, Quakerism for me is not so much a religion but a relationship with God, with myself and with others."

The heart of her faith and her life is that we just love one another. "It is that simple and that difficult." She explores what the word "God" means to her, but says if that doesn't speak to you, don't worry.

She sees perfection as an illusion and asks "what if we could hold the belief that we are good enough just as we are?" In accepting our own incompleteness and weaknesses we can take "the short step to accepting and valuing the imperfections of others."

This book has much food for thought and is a joy to read.
Diana Lampen, Peace educator in Ulster, Belarus and Ukraine

In this exploration of Quaker Faith, Kate McNally weaves together personal experience and reflection. She shows how times of doubt and the development of new insights have both supported her faith, and explains in plain and accessible terms some of the things which have helped her — from the Quaker tradition and beyond. This book is of interest to anyone on a spiritual path, and will be useful to many seekers.
Rhiannon Grant, author of *Quakers do What! Why?*, *Telling the Truth about God*, and *Hearing the Light*

Kate McNally takes us on a clear and cogent deep dive into her Quaker experience, with thoughtful descriptions of Quaker ways of working and being in the world. In contrast to her early church experience, Kate dares to describe a close and personal relationship with God that gives us permission to embrace who we are and the courage to let our lives speak. An engaging read, which I will likely offer to other seekers.

Gretchen Castle, Dean of Earlham School of Religion and former General Secretary of the Friends World Committee for Consultation

QUAKER QUICKS

A Simple Faith in a Complicated World

One Quaker's journey through doubt to faith

QUAKER QUICKS

A Simple Faith in a Complicated World

One Quaker's journey through doubt to faith

Kate McNally

CHRISTIAN ALTERNATIVE
BOOKS

Winchester, UK
Washington, USA

JOHN HUNT PUBLISHING

First published by Christian Alternative Books, 2024
Christian Alternative Books is an imprint of John Hunt Publishing Ltd.,
No. 3 East St., Alresford, Hampshire SO24 9EE, UK
office@jhpbooks.com
www.johnhuntpublishing.com
www.christian-alternative.com

For distributor details and how to order please visit the 'Ordering' section on our website.

ISBN: 978 1 80341 303 7
978 1 80341 304 4 (ebook)
Library of Congress Control Number: 2022940006

A CIP catalogue record for this book is available from the British Library.

Design: Lapiz Digital Services

UK: Printed and bound by CPI Group (UK) Ltd, Croydon, CR0 4YY

We operate a distinctive and ethical publishing philosophy in all areas of our business, from our global network of authors to production and worldwide distribution.

Contents

For Daniel Clarke Flynn: husband, partner, friend. This precious other who is so much a part of me and still so much himself.

Preface

I grew up in a religious family, in a faith that was very dogmatic. I was told what I believed and that if I doubted any of it, I would go to hell. Trying to live that faith felt like hell to me. My response was to throw it all away. But I always believed in a greater good-ness, something more powerful than me, something that was about justice and goodness and fairness. About being connected to a life force. I call that God.

At university I tried out various faiths and couldn't find one whose image of God fit with my own innate sense of God. I stopped looking, and instead turned to psychology and science and the pursuit of success.

This worked for me for a while, providing a measure of comfort but not fulfillment. It fed my ego but not my spirit. At a low point, broken by the drive for success, I began a spiritual journey that has brought me here. Along the way, I found a faith whose idea of God fit with mine or who let me choose my idea of God: the Quakers. It's ironic, because for many years I had joked that if anyone ever held a gun to my head and made me choose a religion it would be Quakers. For me, Quakerism isn't so much about religion as about relationship with God.

So here I am. In order to grow as a Quaker and to respond to the inner voice calling to me I joined a two-year course titled "Equipping for Ministry," designed to deepen our understanding of Quakers and to help find the "right work" for each of us. Over the time of this course, I have found that there is a quiet voice speaking to me, and often *through* me. This book is my way of letting that voice reach the ones who need to hear it.

In Europe, where I live, most Quakers come to Quakerism today as I did: as adults and after searching for a while. This book describes one of the paths that some have followed. If it

1

speaks to you, then it will have done its job. If it doesn't speak to you, then it may be for someone else.

It is important that I say here that I don't speak for Quakers as a whole. I can only describe my own experience. My Quaker community is unprogrammed, which means that we worship in silence, waiting in the stillness to be moved by the Spirit. When that happens we may share what comes to us with others in the meeting; this is called vocal ministry. When we write this down it becomes written ministry. When we let it show in our lives it is living ministry. Much of what you will see here began as written ministry.

Most Quakers in Britain, Ireland and continental Europe and many in the US belong to this unprogrammed tradition. Elsewhere there are also Evangelical Quakers, conservative Quakers and Programmed Quakers, who have different traditions from those described here.

In this book I will necessarily speak of the divine, which I call God. Many Quakers don't use this word, as it has unwelcome connotations. For me, this word connotes a sense of justice, goodness, fairness, and most of all love and even life itself. It's the font from which my work in the world springs. It doesn't matter if you name this "God" or "Spirit" or "Light" or "The Divine." If the word God isn't right for you, please feel free to choose another word that is. Likewise, if this concept of the divine doesn't work for you, please feel free to choose your own.

As Quakers, we believe that we can have direct connection to the divine, and that there is a spark of this divine in all of creation. This connection to the divine is the source and energy and wellspring of the work that Quakers can be called to do. This work can take the form of action in the world or of contemplation. Both are the result of a calling that puts our deep joy at the service of the needs of the world.

There are many paths to faith. This book describes one of them. Parts of it are necessarily personal; most of it is more general, and I hope that all of it is of general interest.

Thank you to all who have supported me in this project from the beginning in small and large ways. I am grateful for your time and thought which made this a better work. This book would not exist without your support: Daniel Clarke Flynn, Andrew Lane, Jennifer Kavanagh, Rhiannon Grant, Paul Hodgkin, Jane Huber-Davies, Lee Taylor, Saskia Kuhlmann, Sean Carroll, Charlotte Allen and Anneke Vliegen. Also Ken Orchard, KL Parker, Paul Hodgkin, Andrew Lane and Daniel Clarke Flynn who are the conscience of my written ministry.

Chapter 1

Questioning, Seeking

My Early Years in Mainstream Religion

When I think about the things I learned about religion as a child, they mostly don't make sense to me. God was interpreted for me, as I was considered not capable of understanding God's glory. I was told that I was born in debt, tainted by the sins of Adam and Eve, who historically did not exist. I had to be redeemed from this sin by the sacrifice of God's own son. I was created imperfect, and the way I was made was somehow not good enough. God created the debt, sacrificed a beloved son to pay it off and yet somehow in the ledger of this all-powerful and all-loving God, the debt lingered. We were told that God loved us, but we still owed God. How to understand this? Who was this God?

It has been said that "God created man in his image and man returned the favor." We imagine God in our own image. I was raised with images of Jesus as a blue-eyed European who looked a little like my brother and God as an old white man standing on a cloud and judging us all. We not only create God in our image, but we also give God the gender of kings.

I believe that these images and the ways in which we interact with them arose in a time and place where rulers needed to be sure of loyalty and fealty to hold on to their power. That power was rooted in the physical power to protect a people from outside threats. Might was right, and so God was imagined as what was needed at that time – the ultimate mighty ruler who would free God's people from whoever was oppressing them. Thus the psalms speak of God protecting us from our enemies, smiting them and leading us to safe places.

Today it is still common to interact with God based on the image of God as a powerful ruler, the king of kings who will destroy our enemies and raise us up to a noble level above others. We worship God and sing praises and continually tell God how great God is. Those who worship God differently are damned by "our" God. This God is demanding and selfish and cruel and will punish us if we don't measure up. And yet we are told that this God loves us, while separating us from our fellow humans.

We know that the common physical images of Jesus and God are not really the right ones and many of us have no problem with re-imagining some of these images. We begin to see reconstructed images of Jesus as he might actually have looked. But how do we feel when we are asked to interact with God differently, in ways that are reflections of a new imagining of God? Not as a powerful ruler who will protect and punish us but as a loving presence who can guide us and show us how to pass that love on to others.

For example, it is expected that we will worship and adore God. The dictionary defines worship as "to pay great honor to" or "to show reverence and adoration for." Literally, to give worth-ship. The origin of the word is Old English, meaning an acknowledgement of the worth of someone. When I think of worshipping God, this definition makes me uncomfortable. Does God really want this? Does God need me to pay honor to God? Does God need me to acknowledge God's worth? It all sounds sycophantic to me if I'm honest.

The Christmas story is another example. Jesus was born to an essentially unwed mother, and it was the poor (shepherds) and the pagans (Magi) who recognized that something wonderful had happened. The powerful ruler sent soldiers to kill the baby.

Did Jesus in the manger need to be worshipped by the Magi, to be told how great he was? Did he really need gold, frankincense and myrrh? In truth, he probably could have used a room at the inn, some clean swaddling clothes and a bodyguard to protect him from Herod.

We are told that we are heirs to the kingdom of God, but that we have to die to enter it. The price of claiming our heritage is that we adhere to a set of rules and strictures here in this world. This life becomes the qualifying round for the big prize that we are told is our birthright – a birthright we can only claim by dying. Meanwhile those who hold the keys to this kingdom seem to have already been able to claim their privileges.

In the church I grew up in we memorized the Apostles' Creed, a statement of the beliefs we held in common. The life of Jesus was only a small part of this creed. Most of it was about the church who held the keys to the mystery. The life of Jesus was described this way: he was "conceived by the holy spirit, born of the virgin Mary, suffered under Pontius Pilate, died and was buried..."

I always felt that this creed ignores the fact that between "born of the virgin Mary" and "suffered under Pontius Pilate" lies the *whole story*. That's where we find the love of God shown in the life of this man who left his family to tell us how much God loves us as we are, to minister to the poor and oppressed, to bring God to the godforsaken.

I often think about Jesus – the man, not the Christ. In my thinking Jesus was a historical person, who lived and died about 2000 years ago. Christ is a title signifying that Jesus was considered to be the messiah, the long-awaited redeemer of mankind who came to save us from sin. Jesus was a human, Christ is a title, never claimed by Jesus. It was not his last name.

When I think about Jesus, I wonder what he was like. For example, what kind of accent did he have and what did that accent say about him? How did he part his hair? What did he call his mom? We hear he was a carpenter—was there one piece he created that he was particularly proud of? Did he like his work? What did he say when he smashed his thumb with a hammer? What was his favorite color? His favorite meal? His favorite swear word? Could he swim? There is so much we do not know about this man and about the things that formed him to be the one we still talk about 2000 years after his death.

I recently visited a church I hadn't visited before, and as is my habit, I lit a candle. As I stood praying, I noticed a nearby statue of Jesus. It's a familiar image, the Sacred Heart, with Jesus pointing to his exposed heart. I wondered if the historical Jesus came into that church at that moment, would he recognize himself in that statue? Would he stop passers-by and point to it, saying "Dude! Look! It's me!"? Would he bring out his phone and take a selfie? Probably not. More likely he'd turn over the table collecting money for the candles and decry the mercantile nature of the church as well as the gold and precious jewels everywhere while there are people homeless on the doorstep of that church.

The religion of my youth had drifted far from this man whose simple message is so needed in the world today. I wanted to find the faith *of* Jesus rather than the faith *about* Jesus. For me it was not possible to find any connection to God in this atmosphere of praise, adoration, gold, jewels and incense.

Chapter 2

Coming Home

For many years, I searched through other religions, looking for the spiritual home that I needed. I could not find it. After years of drifting, I found myself one Sunday morning near a Quaker meeting house shortly before the worship service was to begin. I went in and sat down, engulfed in the silence. This was not silence like any I had known – it was a tangible, living, nourishing thing. I felt that I had found what I had been missing for most of my life, that I was finally home.

Like many convinced Quakers (i.e., those not born into Quaker families or raised as Quakers), I feel that I have always been a Quaker – I just didn't know it. We all have stories to tell about how we found ourselves in a Quaker meeting for worship for the first time, but they all have at their heart this core of a spirit sighing and coming to rest.

When I try to describe Quakers to those unfamiliar with us, it's often difficult to do so without resorting to negatives: We do not have clergy, we do not have any dogma, we do not have hierarchy, we do not believe that any one place is sacred or that God is in any one place unless we bring God to it in ourselves.

I have challenged myself to do this without any negatives, and for me it comes down to this:

- Quakers believe that each one of us can have a direct, unmediated relationship with the divine.
- Quakers believe that each creature has a bit of the divine within.

From these two fundamental beliefs come basic values to be acted on in the world.

Quakers call these *testimonies*:

- *Peace:* We work to bring peace to the world, beginning in our own hearts. We are pacifists: we do not kill the spark of the divine in others. Quakers have long worked for peace in areas of conflict, whether they be war zones, neighborhood battle zones, communities in conflict or troubled individual spirits.
- *Equality:* We believe in equality: the spark of the divine in each of us is the same, and no one person is more important than any other. (We call each other Friend.) Living this testimony means that Quakers work for social justice, notably in the areas of human rights. This shows today as a commitment to anti-racism, as well as work with migrants, LGBTQI rights, women's rights, the rights of prisoners and homeless, and more.
- *Truth and integrity:* We do not misrepresent ourselves or facts to others (i.e., to that spark of the divine in others). This goes beyond just telling the truth, however. It is acting on the deepest truth that we know, knowing that our understanding of truth is necessarily incomplete. It means that we accept responsibility for our actions, and that we speak the truth to others, including to those in power. Quakers do not swear oaths in court, because there should not be a separate standard of truth in court than there is in daily life.
- *Simplicity:* An understanding that we do not own the earth and its gifts. We live in this world as a part of the whole and it must be safeguarded for future generations. We do not use more than we need and we value and challenge materialism. Simplicity is also about non-material things. We free ourselves from the material world in order to give fuller attention to the small voice of God. It is about being more concerned with our inner lives than our outer ones.

As ever with Quakers, it needs to be mentioned that the list of testimonies may vary from one place to another. However, it is always focused on how we live in the world and with each other. These testimonies require that we act in a certain way in relation to ourselves and to each other and to the earth. It is our own understanding, supported by our Quaker community, that guides us in how we respond.

The possibility of every person having a direct relationship with God means that revelation did not stop 2000 years ago. In our silent worship revelation may come to any one of us. While the Bible has a place in the lives of many Quakers, current writings are also relevant. The relative importance of these two for individual Quakers varies depending on their personal beliefs and experience with the divine.

Individual Quaker experiences with God are published in various places and are collected periodically in a book. For British Quakers this book is called *Quaker Faith and Practice*. The current version contains information about the structural organization of British Quakers as well as many chapters describing individual experiences with God. This book is revised periodically, typically once a generation. It contains stories and inspiration that Quakers can refer to as well as other writings that are important. Other more up-to-the-minute sources of Quaker experience are the many and varied Quaker publications that come out weekly, monthly or quarterly.

In the end, Quakerism for me is not so much a religion but a relationship with God, with myself and with others.

Having found this relationship with God, Quakers are often moved to bring the love of God to the world. We are admonished to "Let your lives speak," to work actively for a better world. Some might say that Quakers act on the words of God rather than preach them. This can show up in many ways, but most visibly in the social action by which most people know of Quakers.

Many people know the work of Quakers, even if they don't know much about Quakers themselves. Probably the best-known Quaker projects involve relief work during and after the two world wars. Feeding and providing safety for refugees from the wars garnered Quakers in Britain and the US the Nobel Peace Prize in 1947. The Kindertransport program, which brought thousands of Jewish children and adults out of Nazi Germany, was a Quaker led project. Quakers have also been involved in peacebuilding projects around the world, some well known and others less so. Notable among the places Quakers have worked for peace are Northern Ireland and Palestine.

Quaker values are represented to various governments by Quaker advocacy groups. The Quaker Council for European Affairs (QCEA) represents Quakers at the European Union in Brussels and the Council of Europe in Strasbourg. The Quaker United Nations Offices (QUNO) represent Quakers at the UN in Geneva and New York. Quaker voices are heard in Washington through the Friends Committee on National Legislation (FCNL).

These are the public face of Quakers. But in every community where there is a Quaker meeting, there are grass roots projects which further the cause of our testimonies: peace, equality, truth, simplicity, stewardship. My own work has focused on helping those who have been forced to flee their homes to find safety and a place to build a life as well as dismantling the inherent racism in the western world. When I see the enormous differences between how white European refugees and black African refugees are treated, I am convinced that these two are intricately related.

How do Quakers come to this work? What is the source and wellspring of this need to make the world a little better? For me it has followed a process of connection to God, to myself and to others.

Quaker Roots

Quakerism began in the seventeenth century as a return to early Christianity, to the work of Jesus. In many ways, Quakers continue to do this, to respond to Jesus rather than to the Christ. This means following the one who said that we need to "love one another," rather than the one who is represented in many modern Christian churches. In many ways, Quakers can be said to be called to live in that space missing in the Apostles' Creed between "born of the virgin" and "suffered under Pontius Pilate."

We all agree that Quakerism is rooted in Christianity, but without much explanation or discussion of what that means. In the same way that early Christians were rooted in Judaism, Quakers are rooted in Christianity. It is our spiritual culture, the ground from which we grew, the language and concepts we use to describe our direct experiences with God.

Jesus was rooted in his family, in his culture and in his religion. They informed every aspect of his life. But he also went beyond that culture and even rejected large parts of it.

Our roots nourish us and hold us steady, but we are not our roots. Rather, we grow beyond them. In the same way that early Christians grew from their Jewish roots into something different, Quakers take their Christian roots and grow into something different, which fits our experience with God. These roots sometimes seem to take us back to the origin, to what Jesus said and taught, rather than to the Christ of the Christian churches today.

What does this mean, then? Quakers are mystics, which means that we believe that each of us can have direct relationship with God. The mystical nature of Quakerism means that my experience may not be yours. However, I believe that the roots of Quakerism are not in the cathedrals and the hierarchies of Christianity. I believe that those roots are in the man who taught us to just love one another. It's that simple and that difficult.

In order to be whole and healthy, we need to find connections. To something outside ourselves, to ourselves, and finally to others. Many find these in mainstream religion. I could not.

I believe that in order to be spiritually whole, we need to be able to be in right relation with ourselves, with other people and with God. When these three align, we can be truly in community with others. This is not a new idea, but it is also not one that is in the mainstream of popular thought at the moment.

The religion of my childhood taught us about a Holy Trinity: God the father, son and spirit. Here we will see another trinity: God, self, and others. Connection to and coherence among these three has been the basis of many spiritual programs. There are many paths to the wholeness that this coherence brings. It's in Quakers that I have found it.

Chapter 3

Quaker Practice

Simple Faith

We have a simple faith in a complicated world. We sometimes find ourselves with ethical, practical and moral dilemmas that are historically unique. We do not always know how to proceed.

In times of turmoil we are often in a place between fear and hope, between what we fear will happen and what we hope will be. This is the place of faith, where we find the belief that whatever may be going on at a given moment, it will turn out as it should if we do our part. Sometimes it's not clear what that part may be, sometimes we can see the next step but not the whole path.

Quakers over the centuries have developed practices that help them to understand what the next step might be. These practices are also used to resolve ethical dilemmas and conflicts, to help them live in community and to let their lives speak. Some of these are formal processes, others are individual practices. All of these are based on an awareness of the presence of God, and have the goal of strengthening connections to God, to our true self and to our community.

Practice 1: Holding Someone in the Light

When someone is troubled or suffering, Quakers will often say that they will "hold them in the light." Holding someone in the light feels like wrapping that person in the love of God and letting that love guide them. It feels like sharing the love I find in Quaker worship with someone who may have lost their connection to that love, or maybe they need more than they can find for themselves.

Practice 2: Worship Sharing

Worship sharing at its simplest form is what happens in an unprogrammed Quaker meeting. Friends gather in silence and wait for an inner prompt to speak. Sometimes no one speaks during the time of the meeting. Sometimes many people speak. But generally no one speaks more than once, and no one responds to what another has said. Everyone waits in silence after a contribution in order to absorb what has been said. One contribution may build on an earlier one, but worship sharing is not a discussion or an argument.

Sometimes worship sharing might be agreed as the best tool to explore an issue. In this case, the issue is introduced, Friends gather in the silence and speak when moved to do so. Again, as a general rule no one speaks more than once, and each person makes their own contribution, not agreeing or disagreeing with what has been said before.

Worship sharing as a tool to explore an issue can have surprising results. As we wait in silence, more of the truth is revealed, and each person makes a contribution to the whole, some by speaking aloud and some by upholding the silence.

Practice 3: Clearness

When a decision seems too large to be aided by individual discernment, or when a Friend needs to find clarity on how to respond to a concern, they might ask a group to help them. This "clearness group" can be informally assembled by the individual or more formally appointed by their meeting. However it is assembled, there needs to be absolute trust and confidence in the group chosen. The focus person opens their heart and lays themselves bare and open to the input coming through the others.

The clearness group meets in a spirit of worship sharing, listens deeply, and helps the focus person to make their decision by asking questions without offering answers – only asking.

In my experience there can be a powerful presence of God in these when all can open their hearts to the love that is offered. For the focus person, there is a connection to God, to self and to the group offering support. For the others, the connection to self becomes a channel, allowing the words to come through them, rather than from them.

The focus person doesn't have to know the participants. Some of the most powerful meetings for clearness I have known have happened when one or more of the participants were total strangers to each other. It is only necessary to have the ability to open one's heart and listen without judgment.

Practice 4: Threshing

A threshing session may be called when there is deep division in a meeting about a subject. In the threshing session no decision will be made; rather it is a time for all viewpoints and differences to be aired. This can clear the air for subsequent discernment and decision making. Tried and tested methods for threshing meetings help to make them a safe place to explore disagreement.

Practice 5: Discernment

Discernment is the Quaker process for finding answers. It is a fundamental process, used in many situations. It involves going into the silence and listening for the quiet voice that always tells us the truth. This may come immediately or it may come after some time, but it will only come when we can let go of our agitation and open our hearts to listen. I have heard this process described as "going to center and waiting." Guidance is available.

Individuals may use discernment when a decision has to be made. This can be deciding whether to take on a role in their meeting, or something as simple as deciding if received ministry is for them or for others – to be shared or kept for self.

When Quakers meet to conduct business, issues or concerns which come before the meeting for consideration are also discerned. In collective discernment, Friends try to leave their individual opinions and preferences aside to listen to the Truth that comes in the silence. Here the quiet voice that tells us the truth speaks through the group, reflecting the voice of the whole meeting listening as one. Decisions are not made by voting or by consensus, but by what is called the "sense of the meeting." This refers to a sense of unity around a question which emerges in the course of collective discernment and worship sharing.

Quaker Ministry

Quakers speak of ministry, a word that can take on different meanings in different situations. In a Quaker meeting for worship, someone might be moved to share what has come to them in the silence. This is called vocal ministry. When it takes written form, it is written ministry. When it takes the form of the work we do in the world, it is also ministry. This ministry is often work for which Quakers are most known.

Unprogrammed Quakers do not have designated ministers; rather, we are all charged with ministering to the wounded world. We speak of "the priesthood of all believers," reflecting our belief that we are all called to do God's work. Discovering the work we are called to do is an important task, summed up admirably in the description that it is where our great joy meets the world's needs. I would probably add that our inherent interests and talents are an important part of our great joy.

Chapter 4

Connecting to God

A Word about God

Many Quakers are not comfortable with the word God. Many non-Quakers are the same. As I use the word often in this book, I would like to take a minute to say what it means to me.

How to define the un-definable? How to explain this feeling of intimate connection? Ultimately we each find our own sense of this: an absolute, non-relative measure of life, goodness and justice; a sense of love and connection and the basic force of life. These are my understanding, my words. You will of course choose your own.

I believe that God is in relationships – between inward and outward, between me and you, between them and us, between human and nature. God is a life force that inhabits each of us and which I experience as love, as connected-ness to myself, to others and to (ultimately) everyone and everything.

At one point in my life, I painted, mostly portraits and some landscapes. An artist friend once asked me if I had ever painted God. At that point I had no answer to that. Today I would answer that I painted God in every portrait and in every landscape. When I painted a portrait, it was always from a photo. I looked for photos that showed the person looking inward, absorbed but thoughtful, focused outside and resonating inside. In these unguarded moments, when walls are down, we can see right into the God in someone. That's a holy moment. That's how I painted God.

GOD. I use this word as a shorthand for all of that because it can still bring me a sense of power and awe – not in the old, smite-mine-enemies way, but in a new and deeper way that recognizes the power of this all-enveloping love that has always nourished me no matter what. The word we use to describe this isn't God and the things it describes are not God – rather, they point to God. The word we use to point to this is as good a starting point as any other. We each have to find it ourselves, and to follow the path that is shown to us.

So if the word God doesn't speak to you, don't worry. Feel free to choose your own and substitute it here whenever you see the word "God." You won't be alone – Quakers have a hundred and one ways of naming (and not naming) "God." Quakers are like a family or tribe, with lots of different points of view. We can worship together without needing to have the same beliefs or ideas of the divine.

I live in a country with three official languages, and so the idea of many words pointing to the same thing is a comfortable one for me. In the end, it's not about what you call God or how you define God, it's about how you experience God.

It seems to me that Quakers are less about Christ, who (for me) has come to represent power structures and domination and more about Jesus, who (for me) represents love and service. Understanding this required that I make a journey from my head to my heart. This journey is a long one and involved letting go of many beliefs I had held since childhood.

In the early church creed or dogma was a way to pass the story of Jesus on to those who had not experienced him directly. It replaced direct experience of Jesus and connection to God with connection to the church who mediated divine experiences. Creed, then, grew to include and support the structures of the church and the hierarchy which sustained it.

Quakers moved away from depending on creed and toward experiencing connection to God directly. In Quakers I found a way to replace creedal beliefs with direct experience of the sense of love and justice that I call God. But simply believing in my own experience of God can lead to the arrogance and dogmatism of certainty. So just as important as my direct experience of love and justice is holding this experience within the community of Quakers. This helps me to stay balanced, to hold doubt and love in my heart and to know that it is always possible that I may be mistaken.

How do we connect to God? How do we forge a deep and lasting relationship with the divine? For me, it is through prayer and Quaker worship.

Quaker Worship

A key to this connection is the idea that revelation did not stop 2000 years ago. We each have the ability to connect to the source of divine inspiration today. I find this connection in Quaker worship.

I've mentioned before that I sometimes have a problem with the word "worship" and its literal meaning, which is to give worth to something or someone. My problem is not with the word itself, but with the expectation that we will worship God, i.e., to acknowledge the worth-ship of God, to show admiration for God, and to adore God. Quaker worship in my unprogrammed tradition entails sitting in silence with others waiting expectantly.

The amazing fact of Quaker worship is that we sit in silence not to tell God how great God is (surely God has better things to do than listen to that?). No, in silence together we wait. Sometimes, only sometimes, we feel a connection to God and to the ones around us and if we're very lucky, to ourselves. Our true selves. In Quaker worship we do not find the worth-ship of God, but rather the worth-ship of ourselves. Quaker worship, then, is about opening ourselves to the spirit. It is not about where we go but where we come from.

I do not believe that God cares where I worship or even if I do. I don't think I will find God in meeting houses or churches or holy sites – unless I bring God with me. God doesn't live in sacred places, God lives in sacred actions, in how we treat each other and how we show the love of God in our lives.

At the heart of all Quaker work is listening. Listening in silence, listening to each other, listening to prisoners, listening to migrants, to the homeless, listening to voices that would otherwise be unheard. Actively listening is showing someone their worth. Showing worth-ship to those we listen to. People need this, God doesn't.

We begin this by listening to God. Before we do that, we must listen *for* God. We sit in silence, trying to find stillness, to quiet the inner voices, the noise, the agitation that is the background to our daily lives. When we can do this, we sometimes feel a deepening of the silence. It becomes thicker, almost solid. We feel that we can fall into it and let it support us, wiping away the wounds and scars of daily life. This is a safe and nurturing space where ministry circulates and builds until I hear myself speaking words I don't know until I hear them spoken. There is a spirit there that is precious and nourishing and holy.

Then we understand the mystics, those who dedicate their lives to contemplation, to this connection with the divine essence that is in all of us. Most of us, though, are not chosen for (or by) the contemplative life. We come back to the grind and noise of daily life, cherishing the memory and aftertaste of the feeling of connectedness that is the result of a gathered meeting for worship.

Prayer

Why do we pray? Does God need our advice? Does God need us to direct God's actions, to help decide what's needed (in our opinion...)?

We need that sort of direction sometimes, and if prayer helps us to have it, then it's a valuable action. Sometimes we need help in discerning what is the loving thing to do.

Sometimes prayer feels like bargaining with God, as if God were a vending machine – if we put in enough time on our knees we can get the outcome we would like. Sometimes this sort of prayer can be a letting go of our own expectations and giving up some of the control we think we have over our lives. Sometimes it feels like reminding God that we've kept our part of the bargain and now it's God's turn. Sometimes this sort of prayer reinforces our commitment to the relationship with God. But God is not a puppet master who can be bribed by our good behavior.

Prayer can also be a way of strengthening a relationship with God. What's often missing in discussions of prayer is a prayer of connection to God, of loving God, of the blossoming feeling that I have only found in Quaker worship. I have heard it said that the Jewish name for God, Yahweh, is the sound of breathing: inhale as Yah, exhale as Weh. The first sound we make and the last sound we make is the name of God. Others had said that Yahweh means "I am." I exist and so do you.

C.S. Lewis said that prayer doesn't change God, it changes us. At its best it can remind us that there is a power greater than us and prayer connects us to that power, allowing us to give up control of whatever problems we are wrestling with and trust that we will be okay. It helps us to let go of fear.

Prayer can also be a way of listening to the still small voice that comes to me best in silence. In the opening paragraphs of the Rule of Benedict (the set of rules governing the communal life of Benedictine monks) is written "Listen carefully, my child, to God's voice. Attend to it with the ear of your heart." This is what prayer feels like to me. It feels like inviting God into my daily life.

How do we pray then? And why do we pray?

How:

- With our actions in our life. Our life speaks to the world as well as to God.

- With our words, when we speak to our understanding of God.
- By living with an awareness of the presence of God.
- Learning to tell what's from me *vs* what's through me. When we can take our ego out of it, we can see and hear the leadings of God.
- We go to the center and wait. We listen.
- Why?
- To reinforce connection with God in good and bad times. It's not much of a relationship if it's only there when we need something.
- To invite God into our lives, to direct us in the loving way to act.
- To "tune the receiver" so we can hear the voice of God.
- To be aware for a while of living in the love of God.

God and Accepting our Imperfections

I believe that I was born with a God-size hole in my heart. Seeking God in my childhood church, I found only guilt and not-enough-ness. I was not (and would never be) good enough. I was born tainted by sin, and nothing I could do short of confessing my imperfections and following directions of men who had no idea about my life would make me acceptable to the God who created me. I learned that I had to be perfect to live a godly life. Or at least try to be. Like many others, I spent years in the wilderness of believing that I could not be good enough to earn the love of God.

As a child I had some strange ideas about love. One sort of love was what I called "dearlybut" love. This was because I often heard someone say "I love them dearly, but..." always followed by a criticism. For me, dearlybut love was about criticizing others while saying that you loved them. Another lesson about love came from the oft-repeated "you only hurt the ones you love." Then there was "I'm only doing this (something harsh) because I love you." And my personal favorite, "sex is dirty, so save it for someone you love." The idea that love might be warm and supportive and life-enhancing was a lesson that only came later in life for me.

That began to change when I visited a church whose pastor said that God loves us JUST AS WE ARE. This was something I had never heard before, in church or anywhere else. It was absolutely life changing for me. I broke down in tears. And I could feel an old wound begin to heal.

We all struggle to be perfect, to live up to the perceived perfection of Jesus, to earn the love of God. But does that love need to be earned? What if God loves us just as we are? What if we can learn to accept or even embrace our imperfections?

Perfectionism isn't about trying to be closer to God. It's about trying to BE God. What if we could understand that we are doing our best and that's all that God wants for us? What if we give up the notion of "perfection" and live in our imperfection?

Opening to our true selves means accepting that we are not perfect. But we are perfectly the way we were created to be and our job is to accept that, love that, and use our gifts to bring the kingdom of God to the world.

That also means accepting the imperfection of others, understanding that they too are doing their best to struggle with their imperfect-ness. What if we could love others unconditionally, just as they are? As God does.

Perfectly Imperfect

Many years ago, when I was in graduate school learning to be a psychologist, I took a class that was a little different from most. Buried in the study of psychological abnormalities was a course with the unappealing name of "mental hygiene." It was essentially a class in normal psychology.

Under the guidance of a Freudian psychoanalyst, we studied normal behavior. One day the professor said something that

I will always remember: *normal isn't always healthy, it's just what most people do – it's just average.* We learned that abnormal behavior is most often a simple exaggeration of the normal – a matter of degree.

She went on to say that differences from normal can be a mark of a strong character and are often found in those who make important contributions to their community. Bringing people back into the realm of normal extinguishes the flame of weirdness that makes them special and able to make a difference in the world. To emphasize that point, she said (with a chuckle), "do you realize that if I could have gotten my hands on Jesus Christ he would have been the best carpenter in the world?" We might have gotten a better carpenter but we would not have had the Jesus who changed the world.

In this sense we are all abnormal, imperfect. And that's a good thing. It is our differences from the crowd that let us do the work we are called to do. Our weirdness is also often the thing that helps us to know what that work is.

I think of this sometimes, and am reminded that often the things that most annoy us about others are also the things that enable them to do the work that we admire.

For example, I think of a Friend who is annoyingly persistent when they want something, not taking no for an answer. That fact has allowed them to do amazing things in the local community. In my work with anti-racism, the ability and willingness to be impolite and confrontational is sometimes needed to call out micro (or macro) aggressions. Or to speak truth to power.

We are made the way we are for a reason, and we might think about exploring the usefulness our "not-normality" can bring to our community. We try to get rid of our weirdnesses, but they are also our strengths. We need them to do the work we are called to do.

As Quakers we sometimes celebrate our collective differences from the mainstream, from the normal. Our acceptance of those differences can allow Friends to feel empowered to do work that others shy away from: work with refugees, in prisons, against the arms trade.

Other times we find ourselves uncomfortable with individuals who are different from the Quaker mainstream – those who have a different theology, a different accent or skin color, a different way of approaching our meeting.

What if we could accept our own and others' oddities as an integral part of the gifts they bring to our community? Would that change how we perceive and live with all of those who are not like us? Can we see the gift in the differences among those in our community? Can we show the love of God to those we would like to avoid?

As a Quaker I believe that it is not necessary to be perfect or cleansed or absolved to have a connection with God. It is not necessary to feel love for all of our fellow humans or to be always calm in our spirit. It is only necessary to open our hearts to God and that connection with God will manifest itself.

We connect with people through our imperfection, our human-ness.

God in Other

Our ministry, our "right work," is where our great joy meets the world's needs. We are all imperfect. But we are perfectly suited to the work we are called to do. We can all bring the message of Jesus – that we can and should love one another, that we can and should feed the hungry, tend the sick, bring the kingdom of God to this imperfect world. We are the hands that God has to do this work.

One challenge for Quakers is to take responsibility for our own path, to do the work we need to do to maintain the connection with God which is the source of how we are in the world. We are not spoon-fed beliefs to memorize. Instead we each have to do the hard work of learning how to listen to the divine, to the power and guiding presence that we seek. To keep the receiver tuned.

I believe that to be complete we need to find connection with God (in whatever form or name works for us), with ourselves and with others. Finding God in ourselves demands that we then find God in others to complete the picture.

But first we have to find God in ourselves.

Chapter 5

Connecting to Self

Because of Our Sins

The religion of my youth promised that Jesus will come again. I have always believed that Jesus isn't coming again, because I don't think he ever left. In every generation there are those prophetic voices echoing the message of Jesus: love one another and let your life speak. Often we kill them. Three examples would be Dr. Martin Luther King, Rosa Luxemburg, and Mahatma Gandhi.

In the time of Jesus, crucifixion was a political death – the Roman equivalent of being hanged, drawn and quartered. It was meant to be painful and public and humiliating. It was a warning to those who follow – both those who would come after and those who might already be following the crucified one.

We are told that Jesus died this death for our sins. To redeem us for the sins we have committed and will commit but also for the sins whose burden we carry that were committed by Adam and Eve.

But what if Jesus didn't die *for* our sins but *because of* our sins? Not to balance a ledger but because the sins we carry as humans couldn't let him and his message live?

The sins that were responsible for this particularly cruel and harsh political death are still with us: pride, domination, ambition, control, lust for power, empire. And they are the ones responsible for the continued assassination of those who tell us that we are enough, that we are worthy of love and so is everyone else. They tell us that we should love one another because God loves us just as we are. They tell us that we are all equal and that none are more equal than others. When we can accept this we lose the need to dominate and control others. We also lose the ability to be controlled, which can be a dangerous thing.

Sin separates us from the love of God. These particular sins – pride, domination, ambition, control, lust for power, empire – also separate us from our fellow humans. This separation is part of what enables the dehumanizing process which allows us to kill each other. Every instance of genocide, of war, of cruelty to others begins with this separation into "we" and "them." When "we" separate from "them," it's "them" who generally lose out. And it's this separation that allows us to be controlled by the fear of "them." We might also note that when we separate ourselves from others, God is always on the other side of that separation.

This separation is lost if we can believe that God loves us just as we are, and that is why this message is a threat to those who need for us to be able to kill each other.

The message that God loves us is also the message that we are not separated from God. The radical danger of that message is that if we believe this then we don't need elite power structures to "save" us from ourselves and each other. We only need to know that we are loved and that we can pass that love to others. It's that action of denying/dismantling the power structures that triggers the need to wipe out the one who teaches it, often in cruel and public ways.

I believe that Jesus died not to save us from sin today but because he was saving people at *that* time and in *that* place, as those who are murdered today are saving people in *this* time and in *this* place. The need to dominate and control cannot allow this radical message of love and equality to continue to spread.

What if we could hold the belief that we are good enough just as we are? Could we extend that belief to others – that they are also good enough just as they are? Would we then be able to give up the need to dominate and control others? Could we give up pride and ambition? Could we know that we don't need to accomplish anything more than we have already done? What if we truly loved ourselves and others, as equal recipients of God's grace?

If we could do that we might be able to vanquish the sins which separate us from the love of God and thus cause the death of those who teach us to love one another.

Answering That of God

[Then] you will come to walk cheerfully over the earth, answering that of God in everyone.
George Fox, as quoted in Quaker Faith and Practice of Britain Yearly Meeting, 5th edition, passage 19.32

A Friend recently said that he had had an insight into the phrase "answering that of God in everyone." He said, "There are no exceptions." Of course, I thought, we must answer that of God in those with whom we might be in conflict, or in those with whom we have little in common.

My Friend continued, "and that means answering that of God in myself as well." Oof.

This was a new idea for me, but I think it is an important one. It means that we accept that we are a piece of the whole, that God lives in our hearts too. We tend to think of ourselves as not the same as others, as separate, because we live inside our heads. Answering that of God in ourselves requires that we move from our heads to our hearts, feeling the love that is God and bringing it to the wounded world. It requires that the observer and the observed merge and become one.

The Illusion of Perfection

It is by our 'imperfections' that we move towards each other, towards wholeness of relationship. It is our oddities, our grittiness, the occasions when we hurt or are hurt, that challenge us to a deeper knowledge of each other. Our sins have been said to be stepping-stones to God.

Kenneth C. Barnes, as quoted in Quaker Faith and Practice of Britain Yearly Meeting, 5th edition, passage 21.07

It is said that master carpet weavers purposely introduce an error in their pattern because only God is perfect, and to weave a perfect carpet would be an affront to God.

So much to unpack here. The first thing is the problematic reasoning that says that only God is perfect, and so I have to be sure to be imperfect. This totally ignores the fact that if the first is true the second is not necessary. If only God is perfect, why do I need to be sure to make something imperfect? COULD I make something perfect if I am not God? Presumably not.

So why do we have to go out of our way to make something imperfect? Is there not a kind of hubris here, a sort of spiritual showing off that requires us to wear our piety as a shining garment of forced imperfection?

Then there is the question of why God would need us to be sure to not be perfect. Is God that jealous? It seems to me to be a form of pettiness that is very human and not Godlike at all. We continue to imagine God in human form, with our own imperfections. Which means that the God we imagine cannot be perfect after all.

But for me there is a deeper question. Given that we are created imperfect, what if God sometimes needs us to be perfect? What if one day we have the amazing gift to have a perfect day or to do one thing absolutely perfectly? In the context of our imperfection, one shining example of perfection would be such a gift. Why would we intentionally foul it? Why would we want to not accept it? What does this mean for our relationship with God, with the world?

If we are given this gift of one perfect day we should revel in it. Because it is a gift. A shining moment of grace that comes rarely. More often, we are our normal, imperfect selves. It's in our imperfection that we are fully human and most true to the way we were created. We should strive simply to be our best (imperfect) selves, instead of reaching for the impossible goal of perfection.

What happens to perfect people? Do we really know any? Perhaps a better question is what happens to the ones who are most like Jesus, who try to bring the love of God to the world by working for equality and justice and human rights? What happens to the ones whose work threatens the power structures of the world? Again we might think of MLK, Rosa Luxemburg, Gandhi.

And yet none of these were perfect. We hear stories about our heroes that illuminate their feet of clay. That prove to us that they were not perfect. Often the response to this is to withdraw respect for them and their work. But what if we could understand that they did this amazing work *in spite of* these imperfections? That even with feet of clay they could practice the commandment that we love one another?

Because if they could do their work without being perfect, perhaps we can do our own work too. Our imperfections, our feet of clay, should not prevent us from doing the work we are called to do. It's time to give up the illusion of perfection, which keeps us from achieving our spiritual potential.

Being Our Best Selves

To be loved just as we are is a gift. It is the ultimate acceptance, of us and of the journey we have taken to be who we are. This unconditional love can often trigger an unexpected response: the desire to be our best selves. Being loved for who we are can sometimes inspire us to be better, to return the gift of unconditional love by being more worthy of it. This is not a condition of this love, but it can be a result of it.

Being our best selves requires that we know and acknowledge our strengths and weaknesses. Further, that we explore the ways in which they relate to each other in order to stay as much as possible in the realm of our strengths. This relationship is not always obvious. However, sometimes it becomes clear with a little reflection. For example, I can be confident and I can be organized and I can be persistent. I can also be arrogant, controlling and stubborn.

Exploring the relationships between our strengths and weaknesses shows us that they are often closely related: confidence and arrogance, for example, are two sides of the same coin. So are stubbornness and persistence, being organized and being controlling, being discerning and being judgmental. And so on.

Often we try to get rid of our weaknesses as if they were defects – "quality control" errors or "black spots on our souls."

In fact, we can't do that without getting rid of our strengths as well. They are inextricably linked. We are the way we are made, and granting the gift of persistence also adds the problem of stubbornness. I believe that it's important to realize that our weaknesses are often also our strengths. We need them to do the work we are called to do. We have persistence for a reason – often our challenge is to keep it from hardening into stubbornness. God calls us all, with all of our stuff. It's up to us to understand how to make that stuff useful.

We are not defective. These weaknesses are not defects, but rather patterns of behavior that at one time or another, in one way or another, helped us to survive. Perhaps to survive physically, but more likely to survive psychologically and/or emotionally. They are important to us for that reason. We keep them in our "toolkit" as survival mechanisms, not knowing when or how we might be called on to use them again. But these patterns of behavior also interfere with our relationships: with God, with ourselves, and with other people.

Therein lies our challenge as human beings: to make the best use of these survival mechanisms. To keep our strengths from becoming weaknesses in our everyday lives, where these weaknesses can threaten the links that bind our communities and our relationships with other people.

Because our strengths are also our weaknesses, when we work to eliminate the weakness, we risk eliminating the strength. Instead of trying to eliminate one side of the gift we might instead look for the catalyst that turns a strength into a weakness, the secret ingredient that can turn us from the person we hope or want to be into the one we fear that we are.

I believe that these strengths and weaknesses are related through one thing: fear. Most often, the fear of losing something we have or not getting something we want. When I'm feeling confident and this kind of fear enters the equation, then confidence can slip over a line into arrogance. Conscientiousness can slip into workaholism. Persistence can slip into stubbornness. Organization can slip into control. And so on.

We are called into ministry, into our work in the world, just as we are, with all our stuff. An important part of preparing ourselves for ministry or any important work is to understand our strengths and our weaknesses and how they are related. Because that tells us how to control or minimize the weaknesses to bring out our strengths when we need them. It's the fear that we need to learn to control.

It is up to us to keep on the right side of that line; to keep on the right side of fear. But how can we keep an open heart in a world that daily shows us its cruelty? How can we turn off the fear that makes our strengths into weaknesses and damages our relationships with others? There are many ways to banish this fear, if only for a while.

Because most of the things that I fear are not here with me now, mindfulness exercises can help to dispel the fear that I may not get what I want or that I may lose what I have. Both of those are fears of things in the future. If I can bring myself into the NOW, they lose much of their power.

There are many paths to mindfulness. All have as their ultimate goal to bring us into the present moment and to be aware of the beauty and gifts it offers. One of my favorite exercises involves a small bowl with 36 stones in it. When I find myself full of fear, I empty that bowl and put each stone back in it, thinking of something for which I am grateful with each stone. I can rattle off 10 without thought; 20 is not a stretch. But by the time I get to 36, I am focused absolutely on what is in front of me: the way the light falls on the table, the color of the apple in the fruit bowl, the sound of children's laughter from the park below my window. And then the fear is banished.

But ultimately I believe that the answer lies in faith. Faith that God will bring us through whatever ordeal we are struggling with. Faith that we will have what we need, even if it may not be what we think we need. Faith that we are held in the hand of God and will be okay, no matter what. Faith to take the next step even if we can't see the whole staircase. Faith to do the loving thing, the next right thing.

Where do we find this faith? I find it in Quaker worship.

In Between Spaces

I have spent a lot of time recently thinking about the "in-between" spaces: that pause between inhale and exhale when there is neither; that moment when a ball thrown up is poised between rising and falling; that narrow space between fear and hope which is the place of faith.

When I center down into worship I look for these "in-between" spaces. It's here that I find the opening through which God can enter. It's here that I lose myself and make the possibility of finding something greater than me.

There is another in-between space, not so calm and sacred. It was famously described by Auschwitz survivor and psychotherapist Victor Frankl as the space between stimulus and response. In this space, he tells us, lies our power to choose. And in that choice lies our freedom and our growth. This is a place of possibility and power – the power to choose is the power to change.

Covid lockdown felt like an in-between space for me. Sometimes it felt like the pause between inhale and exhale, or the momentary equilibrium of the ball in the air. But other times (most of the time, really) it felt like a crucible, a place of transformation, a place between nothing and infinite potential. Like Frankl's in-between space, this felt like a place of possibility, a place poised between going forward and going back. What have we made of this, I wonder?

The possibilities for change and transformation were many. On a personal level we might have used this time to learn new skills, to adopt new habits, to mend broken relationships, or to stay the way we were before. On a familial or community level we might have grown closer or we might have fragmented and broken. On a political level we might have unified or divided. On an environmental level we might have gone back into ruin or moved forward into the unknown world of new ways to live. Or perhaps just gone back to a simpler way of life. How have we used this time?

Sometimes I am drawn into worry about the future or about someone I care about. When that happens I find myself in another "in-between" space, this one between the things I hope for and the things I fear. While this space is in reality fairly wide, it can feel very narrow and if I'm not careful I can allow fear to take me in a spiral down into despair. This is the place of uncertainty. It is also the place of faith, where I can find the courage to simply take the next right step.

I've recently been reminded of another Victor Frankl quote, to the effect that it's not important what we expect of life, but rather what life expects of us. He follows that by saying that we should stop asking about the meaning of life. We should instead think of ourselves as being questioned by life. Perhaps this covid "in-between" time is life's way of questioning us, of asking whether we will go forward or back, how we will grasp the possibility of this in-between space.

As Quakers, we are challenged to let our lives speak. As we traverse these "in-between" spaces, how are we transformed? How does the message of our lives speak anew? In the place between fear and hope, how does our faith manifest itself? Do we grasp the possibility and power of these times, or do we squander them? When our lives speak, what do they say?

Perfect Imperfection

Trying to be perfect doesn't get us closer to God. I don't believe that God needs us to be different from how we were created, but only wants us to be our best selves. Our virtues have a dark side. To get rid of our dark side is to also get rid of our virtues, our gifts. We are called to be faithful to our gifts, to manage them, to stay on the lightened side of the divide. On the side of the ocean of lightness rather than the ocean of darkness.

It's our imperfections that help us to connect to other imperfect humans. When we can accept our not perfect-ness we can accept that of others as well. It's our incomplete-ness, our imperfect-ness that means that we rely on others to make our community and our lives whole.

Expecting that we will be perfect can lead us to giving up trying – it's just too hard, and we know that we will fail, by definition. So the expectation that we will be perfect can remove the motivation to try. It also separates us from others. To be perfect is to be isolated, alone.

Accepting our imperfections can ground us in the world, allowing us to live with others in the messy, imperfect world.

This is a game-changing challenge. It means that we have to love ourselves as we are, just as God does. It means that we are good enough, that we give up the too-high bar of perfection as the goal. It means that we can do our best and accept that it will not be perfect.

But can this also be a cop-out? Can we just say, "oh, well, it's not perfect (shrug)"? Perhaps. But it can also open the door to being able to ask for help, to being open to accepting the aid of others whose imperfections are perhaps complementary to ours, making one complete whole. This connection to others is the basis of community, the answer to a basic human need.

That might also mean accepting the imperfection of others, understanding that they too are doing their best to struggle with their imperfect-ness, with staying on the lightened side of their darkness. It might mean that we would need to love others unconditionally, just as they are, with all their imperfections. As God does. In this way we can "answer that of God" in others. We are not called to succeed, but to try.

What would my life be like if I believed in the love of God? If I believed that I am good enough? That it all will be okay, no matter what? What if we could just love one another? Just as we are, as God does.

On Being Happy

Sometimes we are disappointed when our plans are canceled. Listening to the rain patter on the roof is a clear signal that the picnic we had planned is not going to happen. But the much-needed rain can fill the aquifers which give us our drinking water. When we look beyond our disappointment, we can see that we often don't recognize gifts that are given to us, because they don't come in the form we want or expect. Sometimes they come in a different wrapping and so we leave them unopened and unacknowledged. For me, canceled plans might give me future drinking water or the opportunity to spend the day with my husband reading and writing – a gift I hadn't expected.

There is a wonderful phrase in French: *être bien dans sa peau*, which means to be good in one's skin. It means simply to be comfortable with life. This, I think, is what it means to be happy: to walk cheerfully over the world, knowing that we have a place, and to be at peace with the world and with others. I believe that this is our natural state, and that we often block it with fears and resentments and conflict.

We have everything we need to be happy in this life. How do we do it then? How do we find the gifts in the everyday? How do we remove the blocks to being "good in our skin"?

I once had a friend who was always in a good mood, no matter what was going on. She had the gift of finding humor and laughter in whatever life threw at her. I asked her how she did it, and she told me that she had survived a terminal illness several years before I met her. "I'm not supposed to be here," she said, "every day is a gift." How can we find that attitude? Do we have to almost die to be happy?

As I look at the people in my life who are truly happy, it's not the ones who have the most or the ones who have the easiest lives. It's often the ones who have the least and who have been through ordeals that I don't know if I could survive who have found the key to being good in their skin.

Someone once told me that there's a difference between wanting to be happy and choosing to be happy. One of them is an action. It seems easy enough, but it's not. I can't hold my breath and just be happy. It takes some work.

First I have to let go of some things:

- *expectations*, which only set us up for disappointment or resentment

- *entitlement*, which tells us that we deserve more than our share
- *judgment*, which tells us that we are better than others
- *comparing ourselves to others*, using others as the benchmark we aim for
- *jealousy*, believing that we deserve what others have and that their good fortune should have been ours
- *the need to be special*, or better than others
- *perfectionism*, where we try to be like God
- *toxic relationships*, which confirm all our worst fears about ourselves

These are all things that separate me from other people, isolating me in my tiny mind – truly a bad neighborhood.

Then I have to find some things:

- *acceptance* – I stop fighting what I can't change
- *connection*: to self, to God, to others. It is the connection to others that I most missed in covid times.
- *joy* – which flows from the feeling of connection.

Then I have to give some things away:

- *love* – in order to have it you have to give it away
- *things/possessions/money*, these are no more than tools for the work God calls us to do
- *time* – the span of my life is measured in time. I give it away by spending it, making the world a little better for others. Or maybe just making my small corner of it better. Letting my life speak.

This is not an easy path to walk. It gets narrower and narrower as we go along. Once we set our feet on it we are drawn along trying not to be distracted by the side-turnings. Often I fail. But sometimes, just sometimes, it works.

Chapter 6

Connecting to Others

Our life is love, and peace, and tenderness; and bearing one with another, and forgiving one another and not laying accusations one against another; but praying one for another and helping one another up with a tender hand.
Isaac Pennington, 1667, as quoted in Quaker Faith and Practice of Britain Yearly Meeting, 5th edition, passage 10.01

At the heart of faith is community, the safe nurturing space where we can be truly ourselves, accepted with all of our faults and all our gifts. In order to create this, I believe that we need to first know ourselves deeply and honestly, warts and all. If we can accept ourselves as we are, we can begin to accept others as they are as well, and there begins community.

It's our incompleteness, our weaknesses, if you will, that force us to break the isolation of ego and reach out to others with whom we can be complete. In an ideal world, we would all live happily with our brethren, the lion would lie down with the lamb and the strains of *kumbaya* would drift over it all. Sadly (or not, depending on how you feel about *kumbaya*) this is not the case.

Despite our best efforts, living in community with others isn't always easy. It will inevitably lead to conflict. After all, it's the rough edges that make a diamond sparkle, and it's a hard truth that when we live with others we will inevitably rub against their rough edges. And they will rub up against ours. For all the peacebuilding skills that Quakers try to cultivate, every Quaker community has trouble from time to time living these principles. Because we are all human and therefore imperfect.

In the past, Friends could be "read out of meeting," or shunned for violations of Quaker values such as listening to music or dancing or marrying a non-Quaker. While this practice has fallen by the wayside, Quakers today are not immune to the temptation to judge each other. We apply the term "unquakerly" to those who we believe don't measure up to our standards. We ostracize or "other" those with whom we are not comfortable.

But we sometimes forget that the voice that we hear judging others is the same voice that we hear judging ourselves. We can never satisfy it until we learn to accept our imperfections. Quieting that voice lets us accept and even value our imperfections. From there it can be a short step to accepting and valuing the imperfections of others.

Judging others, with the inevitable feeling of superiority that it brings, separates us from them. It also separates us from God, who is manifest in the ones we judge. It gives power to the voice that judges us and which usually finds us below par. As we find others lacking, we also find ourselves lacking.

Giving up the satisfaction of judging others allows us to give up the torment of judging ourselves. Giving up the measuring stick of perfection allows us to see others (and ourselves) as multi-faceted, multi-talented and valuable just as we are. I would like to be better at this than I am. I do my best but don't always succeed. I can only hope for upward progress, spiraling toward wholeness.

The mystical nature of Quakerism means that we each must find our own way, supported by our community. This combination of individual responsibility and group guidance can sometimes lead to conflict.

Dealing with conflict is a basic human skill, part of the human condition. We can avoid it, we can manage it, we can resolve it. But we cannot eliminate it. Living in community requires that we learn to resolve our conflicts before they break our community apart. This often means speaking TO each other rather than ABOUT each other. It means speaking honestly and openly about the situation, accepting our imperfections as well as those of others, and enjoying the differences among us.

It also requires a lot of forgiveness.

Forgiveness

Who doesn't seek it? Who doesn't need it? How do we get it? We all carry around resentments, wounds that impair our ability to function as a whole person.

There is a story that the author Corrie ten Boom was asked to forgive one of the Nazi guards from Ravensbruck, the prison camp where she and her sister were imprisoned and where her sister died. She found that she wasn't able to do it. She prayed to be given the strength, and at the moment she committed to making the effort she reported that she was filled with a healing warmth that she called the love of God.

In *The Merchant of Venice* Shakespeare tells us "in the course of justice, none of us should see salvation. We do pray for mercy, and that same prayer doth teach us all to render the deeds of mercy. In that prayer we ask, "forgive us our trespasses AS we forgive those who trespass against us."

This can be understood as meaning "in the same manner" as we forgive others. To the extent that we can completely forgive someone else we can be completely forgiven. If the best we can summon up is incomplete and grudging forgiveness that's what we find for ourselves. Our forgiveness of others is a prerequisite for being forgiven ourselves.

"As we forgive others" can also be understood as meaning "at the same time" as we forgive others. It's a simultaneous process of healing *which we initiate*. Francis of Assisi is credited with saying "it is in pardoning that we are pardoned." I think that this is what Corrie ten Boom experienced. It's an interlocking action. Or is it the same one? Is forgiving others the same as forgiving ourselves?

I believe that what Quakers call "that of God" within me forgives me and that flows outward to forgive you. In order for this to happen, we need to give up our identity as the wounded one and find a new identity that recognizes "that of God" in everyone. We need to ask ourselves who we can be without that woundedness.

The moment when we are able to give up our identity as the wounded one is the moment we are made whole. To keep this wholeness we must allow it in others as well. I believe that the Quaker testimony of equality starts here.

When we learn to forgive ourselves for not being perfect, we must next learn to apply that to others. When we learn to believe that we are doing the best we can do, we must grant that same effort to others: we must also believe that they are doing their best. When we can live in that truth, we can let go of the need to judge or punish others and then ourselves. This is how we find peace.

When we can forgive ourselves for our imperfections, accept them and understand how to deal with them, we can be "good in our skin." Then we can also understand that others are imperfect, as they were created, and also trying their best. Fear is working in their lives too. Sometimes it may be a fear of *our* actions which drives them to unusual behavior and which in turn damages our relationship with them. Just as our own fear of their actions damages that relationship. When we fully understand this, we feel a connection to them, human to human, imperfection to imperfection.

When we can forgive ourselves we can understand that all of us are (normally) doing our best. When we fall short it's because we let the fear turn our strengths into weaknesses, our good to harm. When faith enters the picture, along with the humility to ask for help and admit wrong, then we can leave the hell of believing we are not good enough or blaming others for our actions.

A New Use for Quaker Tools?

Sometimes it's not so easy to find the grace to forgive others (or ourselves), and unresolved conflict can destroy our Quaker communities. Often there is work to do to ready us to forgive each other. Earlier, we saw the tools that Quakers have developed to help to resolve ethical dilemmas and to find the way forward when it is not clear. These tools are designed to help us to re-connect with others and prepare us to work together on whatever the particular project may be, whether forgiveness or marriage or refugee housing. They are also useful when there is conflict in the Quaker community.

These are not the same as the tools often used to resolve conflict, and in fact, these tools are not specifically designed to be used in conflict situations. However, they can be used to walk a middle path, designed not so much to resolve the conflict as to reconnect the conflicting parties with each other so that the conflict can be dealt with in a loving way.

Resolving conflict often means ignoring what is in our heads and focusing on what is in our hearts. Forgiveness happens in a heart space we create between us. We listen intently to another person sharing the pain that has created conflict and we share our pain in the same space. If we can each hold that space for the other, we have a chance to let go of the pain and find resolution.

Worship sharing: Hearing the other in mutually created shared space is at the heart of much of the work that Quakers do. We listen and then take what we have heard into the silence where we wait for the still small voice that helps us see the truth. When that voice has spoken, we share our truth and the other takes it into the silence and waits. This requires that we create a silence in which we are willing to open our hearts, to share the pain that is the core of conflict, to own our part in it and to listen to hear the pain of the other.

We cannot begin to let go of the pain and separation of a conflict if we do not feel that we have been heard.

Clearness: Sometimes we need to make a decision or clarify an issue in our hearts before we can move forward to connect with others. For this, Quakers sometimes use a Clearness process. While this is most often used in non-conflict situations, it can help to clarify exactly what is the source of the pain and separation at the root of the conflict.

Clearness can also help us to connect to the clearness group in a way that can lead us to open our hearts in a situation more directly related to the conflict. We need people we trust to hold up a mirror to us so that we can see through the walls we have built to protect ourselves. It's only when we feel safe and nurtured that we can begin to take down those walls. Clearness groups can be that mirror for us.

Discernment: Here we understand the will of God by going to the center and waiting. In the silence we will hear the promptings of the spirit. Again, not a tool specifically designed for conflict situations, but useful in almost all aspects of Quaker life. We use discernment to help us to know what is the loving thing to do when we are not sure. We can also use it to help us to respond to that of God in someone with whom we are in conflict.

Discernment can help us to know ourselves: when we know our demons we can recognize when they are at work in our lives. Patterns of conflict over similar issues point back to us and to work we need to do.

I once had a mentor in my corporate life who would listen patiently while I related the details of whatever conflict was plaguing me at the time. She would then ask me to tell her the story from the point of view of the other person. Because, she said, nobody wakes up in the morning, looks in the mirror and tells themselves that they are going to be "unpleasant" that day (she may have used a stronger word). In order to begin to find a way out of the problem I had to be able to see it from another point of view.

This is one of the things that discernment can do: to see the point of view of the other person in our conflict, to humanize them and to focus on the different perceptions of the situation rather than the pain we are feeling about it.

Connecting to Others in Quaker Worship

Do you try to set aside times of quiet for openness to the Holy Spirit? All of us need to find a way into silence which allows us to deepen our awareness of the divine and to find the inward source of our strength. Seek to know an inward stillness, even amid the activities of daily life. Do you encourage in yourself and in others a habit of dependence on God's guidance for each day? Hold yourself and others in the Light, knowing that all are cherished by God.
Advices and Queries #3 in Quaker Faith and Practice of Britain Yearly Meeting, 5th edition

Quaker worship feels to me like sitting still in the love of God, feeling that connection to the eternal that takes me out of time and place and into a sense of fullness, of completeness.

I don't feel this in the busy noise of church rituals. Sometimes I find it in the silence of nature, of the forest or the fens, but most often worshipping with those Quakers in whose safe and nurturing presence my heart can rest.

Then I feel a flow of love that calms my spirit and awakens in me a sense of the universal. I believe that this flow of the love of God is something that goes on all the time; we just dip in and out, and can feel it when we let our walls down and open ourselves to the love of God.

This sense of being in that perfect love feels like a fragile thing. Feeling this love seems like only half the work: the rest is to bring it back to the world. When we can bring the love of God back to the world we can fulfill the ministry that brings our great joy to the needs of the imperfect world. The trick is to keep holding on to that love, that feeling of absolute peace and presence that comes when worship happens.

Often I fail. It's hard to bring it back into the world of humans elbowing each other for prestige and recognition and wealth and power without putting up the fences and walls that I use to protect myself from a world that seems to have forgotten this amazing feeling of connection. Those walls and fences of self-defense bind up the flow of love and thus kill it. It needs to circulate. We only keep it by giving it away.

But what if we could trust that sense of peace and presence? What if we could come back to the world and lay down those walls? Just live wide open?

Living wide open is hard to achieve where there is judgment or conflict or unresolved issues. Whether judgment and conflict are in our personal lives or in the greater world, they can block us from God's love. Not because God doesn't love us, but because they generate fear which clogs the channel through which that love flows. The simple admonition to "love one another" holds the key to holding on to that sense of completeness and connection in a world that seems to be falling apart. It tells us to bring back the love of God that we find in worship and to give it away, especially to those who need it most.

Love one another. It's that simple and that difficult.

I keep saying that. "Love one another." Is it really that important for Quakers? I believe it is, because we need others to complete our experience of God. We all have a spark of God in us. It may be incomplete. In order to experience God more fully we need to add our spark to those of others.

When I was a professor of psychology, I used to teach about Freud, Maslow, James, Jung, Erikson, and Piaget. Also Pavlov, Skinner, Tinbergen and Sherrington. Students, frustrated by all the explanations for human behavior, used to ask, "which of these theories is true?" The answer is that they are all true — but they are incomplete. All of these psychologists are looking at the same thing: Human behavior (overt, covert, cognitive, etc.). And they are trying to explain it. They naturally understand it from the point of view of a lens formed by their own experience. For them this is enough. Each contributes a little bit more to our overall understanding of the subject of psychology, which is ultimately human behavior in all its forms. In order to understand it better we need more input, from each of these and from others yet to come.

I believe it's the same for Quakers. Some are Christian, some are Jewish, some are Pantheist, some are non-theist. We are all looking through the lens of our own experience for something that transcends ourselves. We all can contribute to a larger understanding of the divine, but only if we can share in a safe and nurturing space. Our own view is certainly enough for many of us, but I believe in order to truly understand or experience God we need not only our own unmediated experience, but also that of others, which naturally comes to and from a different perspective. *We* are stronger in this than *I* am. This is what we search for in a spiritual community.

Achieving this requires that we let go of what blocks the flow of experience of God – not just individually, but as a community. I believe that fear and judgment of others are at the root of many of the fractures in our spiritual communities and that we need to let go of judgment and the separation it causes.

Judgment and My Bath Towel

When I think about judging others I sometimes think of my bath towel. It is at least 25 years old. It was once white, but is now a nice Quaker gray. I love this towel. We have history. It has been with me through many trials and tribulations, and I use it often. The main thing that I love about it is that if I wash it and let it air dry it will be very rough and scratchy. When I use it to dry my back, it gives me a lovely back scratch. If I put it over the radiator while I take my bath it envelops me in a warm hug when I get out.

I have other towels. They have bright colors and naturally indwelling fabric softeners. I confess that when we have company I often put those out instead of my old gray one. Often, but not always. If the company is someone who doesn't judge or someone I love and trust, I will leave the gray one out on the hook. Houseguests always get the nice ones. Likewise, my house is cleanest when the guests are not my favorite people. This is not necessarily something I am proud to say.

Why is this? I believe that it is because the ones we trust the most are also the ones who know us and love us just as we are, imperfect. These are the people we let into our world, where we can let down the barriers and the walls we live behind. When we can let down our walls, we can acknowledge our Quaker towels – those much-loved but no longer perfect parts of ourselves that we may be reluctant to put on display. When we live in a nurturing community, we live in a state of much-loved imperfection.

In worship we practice being centered and fully present. We learn to love ourselves and then our neighbor, and then our neighbor as ourselves.

As ourselves not as someone or something else. As our true selves. Not as who we want to be, not as who we want others to think we are, not as who they think we are, or as who they want us to be. Or as they see us. But who we really are: imperfect, gifted and flawed, trying our best, trying to do better, trying the patience of others.

Can we love our neighbor truly? We have to stand and live according to our nature. And so do they.

Chapter 7

Letting Our Lives Speak

The love of God guides me to do one thing: to share that with other people. How I do that depends on what's going on around me. My job is to take that love and bring it back to the world.
Delson Malumbe, Quaker in Congo. Personal communication

Quakers in community, working together, worshipping together, have always felt the call to "let your life speak." To bring the love of God found in worship back to the world to make it a little better. To do their best to bring the kingdom of God to this broken world.

In short, to love one another.

For many Friends, "Quaker" is a verb. There is a momentum that begins in meeting for worship and propels us to work in the world. For these Friends, Quakerism is a practice. It's not just for Sundays anymore, it's for life every day. To live in a wholly holy way by sharing the love of God with the imperfect world.

Where does this compulsion to change the world come from? I believe it comes from the connection to God found in Quaker worship. We wrap ourselves in the love of God and then bring it back to the world around us.

From the beginning in the seventeenth century, Quakers have let their lives speak through living ministry, through action which springs from a connection to God and to Quaker testimonies. Mentioned earlier are the Kindertransport program and Quaker work with refugees in Europe after WWII. Beyond these, Quakers were among the founders of Greenpeace and Amnesty International, EPLO (European Peace Liaison Organization) and others. Quakers are often involved in many smaller projects enriching local communities.

I can't claim to be an expert on the Bible, but I'm pretty sure that Jesus never said "pick up your cross and worship me." I think what he said was "follow me – do what I do: tend the sick, feed the hungry, welcome the stranger." I believe that the Quaker form of worship helps us to connect to our deeper selves and then go beyond them to "let our lives speak"; to work for the world we want to see.

Eventually, life asks each of us who we are. How can we reply? When our life speaks (as it inevitably does), what will it say?

Some people find God in mystery, in unattainable aspirations, in seeking perfection. But that's not where I find God. That's where I think I *am* God. Trying to be perfect is trying to be God. It's in our imperfection that we find the difference between us and God. I find God in other people. That's where we find our humanity.

When we accept our imperfection we can bring the message of Jesus – that we can and should love one another, feed the hungry, tend the sick and thereby bring the kingdom of God to this imperfect world. I have said before that I do not find God in holy places or even in meeting for worship very often. I find God in the actions that let my life and the lives of others speak. I believe that Jesus isn't present in the ones who feed the hungry or in the hungry who are fed. Rather, he is present in the *action* of feeding them – the action that binds them together in a connection that is godly.

God lives in sacred actions, in how we treat each other and how we show the love of God in our lives. This action connects us one to another and in that way forms a perfect-ness that neither person can bring alone.

A Ministry of Presence

In Quaker worship I sometimes hear or feel a voice saying, "I'm here." It's enough. It's the foundation of the rest. It frees my soul and makes it sing. My heart swells with it.

Sometimes Quaker work takes the form of simply being there, of saying "I am here," "I see you," "you are loved and important." These are holy words, words of comfort. They help us to let go of the burden of self and join with another.

Accompaniment is one way that Friends let their lives speak, to simply say "I'm here." Examples are:

- Prison ministry, where Friends sit with imprisoned people and recognize their humanity.
- Humanitarian accompaniment, where Friends walk alongside those in danger or in sorrow. One example of this is the EAPPI program, (Ecumenical Accompaniment Program in Palestine and Israel), which sends humanitarian observers to Palestine to observe and report on the interactions between Palestinians and Israelis.
- Silent witness, where Friends simply stand in witness of wrongs in society. An example is silent protest outside Arms Fairs and military sites.
- Sitting with another person who is in distress, to simply listen. To say "I'm here, listening. I see you, I hear you, I see this."
- Sometimes it's as simple as in the depths of night when my husband wraps his arms around me and whispers "I'm here."

God's Hands: a Personal Calling

The covid pandemic showed how many of us need love to drive out the fear that grew up around us in those years. We all need love to quench the fires of fear and dread and the grief we feel for parts of our lives that are lost to us. How can we provide this for others when the love we need to find is drowned out by our own fear? How can we awake the faith that we need in order to do God's work, to drive out fear with love when our own reservoir of love feels so depleted?

We can remember that the love that comes *from* us is finite. The love that comes *through* us is infinite. The prayer of St. Francis reminds us that we can be a channel of God's love for others. It's up to us to keep that channel open, to not clog it with fear and anxiety and grief.

It's not only our family and friends who need our love to make their way in the world. Everyone we see is carrying the burden of difficult times, in different ways and with differing levels of success.

I see this most clearly with strangers who need loving support. For the past five years I have worked with others to support people forced to flee their homes and families. Not in large numbers, normally one or two at a time. They come to us having suffered all of the hellish things we hear about on the migrant routes. We see people who have escaped genocide, crossed the Sahara and been enslaved in Libya. They have lost friends crossing the Mediterranean, then crossed all the borders in Europe to get to Belgium, and we support them in this step of their journey.

And then, they move on.

It's hard to see them go into the Channel, where we hope they reach England. And yet I've come to know that these are not my children, they're God's children and they're in God's hands. They always have been.

For the part of their journey that is here in Belgium, we are God's hands, and then we send them on; they will stay in God's hands and they will stay God's children. We just do our part here. Sometimes we can send them on into God's hands in the form of other Quakers. Sometimes we can only send them on, but we send them on always as God's children.

It's an important part of my Quaker faith to bring God's hands here to people who need it and just to know that it is good enough. That's all I can do. I can't follow them. I can't protect them, I can't guarantee them success. I have to release them back into those hands that brought them here.

In the same way, I think it is also important to remember that our loved ones who are suffering from fear and grief are also God's children. They may be lent to us, but they are ultimately God's. We channel God's love to them, and then let them go.

We have to find our faith – our faith that we will find the resources we need: financial, physical, spiritual, personal. That we will find the people who can help with the work when we need them, and that we will have the support we need to help our loved ones on to the next part of their journey; that we will be able to follow Jesus in the work he began: love one another.

When that happens, we have our marching orders: "pick up your cross and follow me." The message is clear: not "worship me," but "follow me." Feed the hungry, tend the sick, welcome the stranger, let your life speak. Take the love you've been given unconditionally and pass it on. Give it to others who need it, who need to feel that miraculous connection that was given to you. This is the way I am called to serve. Others are called to serve in other ways.

I believe that bringing the kingdom of God to earth is about bringing the love of God to the earth. One person, one action at a time.

This might be a place to make a plea for self-care. Bringing the kingdom of God to the godforsaken world can be psychologically dangerous. Each little bit of grief takes its toll until we are empty. But the next person who comes to us needs us to be able to give them all we can. They need us whole. We can't carry someone else's load permanently – we have to give it back to them or lay it down.

It's probably also important to remember that we can't bring Jesus to the poor, to the oppressed. Jesus is already there. We have to bring Jesus to our own hearts. Then we will know how to help those who need us.

The range of Quaker work in the world is immense. Quakers can be found working in all parts of the world, on all sorts of issues. Most of this work can be categorized under our testimonies, working to bring peace, equality, truth and simplicity to the world today.

The list of Quaker projects is long and always changing. To have an idea of how Friends let their lives speak, check out the following websites:

Britain: https://quaker.org.uk/our-work/our-stories

Ireland: https://quakers-in-ireland.ie/about-us/concerns/

US: https://www.afsc.org/key-issues

Europe and Middle East: https://fwccemes.org/emes/peace-and-service-consultation

And finally, to find out more about Quakers where you live see: https://fwcc.world

We have a simple faith in a complicated world. I believe it gives us a way to connect to God, to that of God in ourselves, and ultimately to that of God in others. In this way we can find the union with God and others that is our birthright as human beings.

A psychologist by training, Kate McNally worked as a university professor and as a management consultant in the US and Canada. In 2001 she and her husband, Dan Flynn, moved to Belgium where she taught English to businesspeople and became a Quaker. She has represented Quakers at the Council of Europe and worked with the Quaker Council for European Affairs on projects related to forced migration, racism, and vicarious trauma among humanitarian aid workers. She is an elder and associate tutor at Woodbrooke Quaker Study Centre where she teaches courses on anti-racism. She is a frequent contributor to the British magazine *The Friend* and is a certified chocolate taster and judge. She blogs at http://bravespaces.blog

Also in this series

Quaker Quicks - Practical Mystics
Quaker Faith in Action
Jennifer Kavanagh
ISBN: 978-1-78904-279-5

Quaker Quicks - Hearing the Light
The core of Quaker theology
Rhiannon Grant
ISBN: 978-1-78904-504-8

Quaker Quicks - In STEP with Quaker Testimony
Simplicity, Truth, Equality and Peace - inspired by Margaret Fell's
writings
Joanna Godfrey Wood
ISBN: 978-1-78904-577-2

Quaker Quicks - Telling the Truth About
God Quaker approaches to theology
Rhiannon Grant
ISBN: 978-1-78904-081-4

Quaker Quicks - Money and Soul
Quaker Faith and Practice and the Economy
Pamela Haines
ISBN: 978-1-78904-089-0

Quaker Quicks - Hope and Witness in Dangerous Times Lessons
from the Quakers On Blending Faith, Daily Life, and Activism
J. Brent Bill
ISBN: 978-1-78904-619-9

Quaker Quicks - In Search of Stillness
Using a simple meditation to find inner peace
Joanna Godfrey Wood
ISBN: 978-1-78904-707-3

CHRISTIAN ALTERNATIVE
BOOKS

THE NEW OPEN SPACES

Throughout the two thousand years of Christian tradition there have been, and still are, groups and individuals that exist in the margins and upon the edge of faith. But in Christianity's contrapuntal history it has often been these outcasts and pioneers that have forged contemporary orthodoxy out of former radicalism as belief evolves to engage with and encompass the ever-changing social and scientific realities. Real faith lies not in the comfortable certainties of the Orthodox, but somewhere in a half-glimpsed hinterland on the dirt track to Emmaus, where the Death of God meets the Resurrection, where the supernatural Christ meets the historical Jesus, and where the revolution liberates both the oppressed and the oppressors.

Welcome to Christian Alternative... a space at the edge where the light shines through.
If you have enjoyed this book, why not tell other readers by posting a review on your preferred book site.

Recent bestsellers from Christian Alternative are:

Bread Not Stones
The Autobiography of An Eventful
Life Una Kroll
The spiritual autobiography of a truly remarkable woman
and a history of the struggle for ordination in the Church of
England.
Paperback: 978-1-78279-804-0 ebook: 978-1-78279-805-7

The Quaker Way
A Rediscovery
Rex Ambler
Although fairly well known, Quakerism is not well understood.
The purpose of this book is to explain how Quakerism works as
a spiritual practice.
Paperback: 978-1-78099-657-8 ebook: 978-1-78099-658-5

Blue Sky God
The Evolution of Science and Christianity
Don MacGregor
Quantum consciousness, morphic fields and blue-sky
thinking about God and Jesus the Christ.
Paperback: 978-1-84694-937-1 ebook: 978-1-84694-938-8

Celtic Wheel of the Year
Tess Ward
An original and inspiring selection of prayers combining
Christian and Celtic Pagan traditions, and interweaving their
calendars into a single pattern of prayer for every morning and
night of the year.
Paperback: 978-1-90504-795-6

Christian Atheist

Belonging without Believing

Brian Mountford

Christian Atheists don't believe in God but miss him:
especially the transcendent beauty of his music, language,
ethics, and community.

Paperback: 978-1-84694-439-0 ebook: 978-1-84694-929-6

Compassion Or Apocalypse?

A Comprehensible Guide to the Thoughts of René Girard

James Warren

How René Girard changes the way we think about God and the
Bible, and its relevance for our apocalypse-threatened world.

Paperback: 978-1-78279-073-0 ebook: 978-1-78279-072-3

Diary Of A Gay Priest

The Tightrope Walker

Rev. Dr. Malcolm Johnson

Full of anecdotes and amusing stories, but the Church is still a
dangerous place for a gay priest.

Paperback: 978-1-78279-002-0 ebook: 978-1-78099-999-9

Readers of ebooks can buy or view any of these bestsellers by
clicking on the live link in the title. Most titles are published
in paperback and as an ebook. Paperbacks are available in
traditional bookshops. Both print and ebook formats are
available online.

Find more titles and sign up to our readers' newsletter at
http://www.johnhuntpublishing.com/christianity
Follow us on Facebook at
https://www.facebook.com/ChristianAlternative